Twelve Traits of a Ninja

Live Like a Ninja

Traits that will improve your life

THE HEART OF A NINJA SERIES

Also by Chris Warnky

The Heart of a Ninja: Stretch Your Boundaries

What Just Happened?: The Line

What Just Happened?: The Run

The Heart of a Ninja for Kids

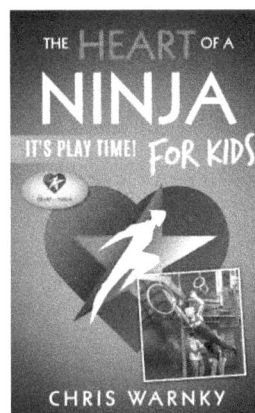

Twelve Traits of a Ninja

Ninja

Live Like a Ninja

Chris Warnky

Well Done Life LLC

Columbus, Ohio

2019

Well Done Life

Chris Warnky/Well Done Life LLC
1440 Mentor Drive
Westerville, Ohio 43081

Editor: Gwen Hoffnagle
Cover Layout by Fiverr pro_ebookcovers
Book Layout © 2017 BookDesignTemplates.com

Ordering Information:
Quantity sales: Special discounts are available on quantity purchases by corporations, associations, and others. For details contact "Special Sales" at the above address.

Twelve Traits of a Ninja: Live Like a Ninja / Chris Warnky – 1st ed.
ISBN 978-0-9993331-6-7

Dedication

This book is dedicated to our awesome and amazing Creator/God. Thank you for allowing me to live a very blessed first 62 years of my life.

It's also dedicated to all those who are thinking about, already training for, and maybe dreaming of one day getting to compete in a ninja competition or even be on *American Ninja Warrior*.

Contents

Introduction

I wrote *Twelve Traits of a Ninja* to challenge you to think better about your choices and to encourage you to get out and move and play in the ninja world playground that I've found to be so fun. I hope to do this through sharing my experiences, stories, and example. I dream that thousands of you will make better life decisions and physically move and play more, which will improve your lives.

I Won and Gained the Heart of a Ninja

I developed the heart of a ninja over the past five years. I feel younger than I did when I started at age 57. I have won in the way that I've lived my life, spending significant time in ninja activities: moving, playing, gaining strength and balance, and learning and growing as a person. *American Ninja Warrior* (*ANW*) boldly moved into my life and helped make me a better person.

Twelve Traits of a Ninja was written for those who love *ANW*, those who want to become a ninja, and those who are starting their ninja journey. It's especially for those of you who have said, either in your mind or even out loud, "I could do that!" or "Wow, I could never do that!" I share some insights about my training experience that I hope you will find interesting and motivating. As you read, I hope you enjoy this ride as much as I have.

Play

Play is when we get creative and set up a game-like environment in which we strive to win. It might be trying to beat our prior best performance in an activity, doing it better or faster. Play includes the excitement and anticipation of success or failure, and the thrill of pushing ourselves as far as we can go, like running as hard as we can, zigging and zagging to tag someone in a game of tag, or maybe doing our best to avoid being tagged. Play is a fun, safe environment in which it doesn't really matter whether we win or lose. It's a healthy aspect of life. We don't have to play all the time, but we can benefit from playing often.

Becoming a Ninja

Just a few years ago, I had never heard of *ANW*. *Sasuke*, which is the original version of ninja warrior, was a big deal in Japan and had been for years, and *ANW* had already made a big splash in the United States on the G4 television network. I was introduced to *ANW* by my daughter, Michelle, and my wife, Carolyn, in 2012, during *ANW* season four.

When Did My Ninja Journey Begin?

I remember back to my fourth-grade class at Mount Pleasant Grade School in St. Louis, Missouri. The bell rings and it's recess time. Yay! It's one of those recesses when I'm not staying inside writing sentences because I was talking during class. It's a warm and sunny day and I get to play on the playground, the monkey bars, or what we called the jungle gym. It's so much fun to climb across it, walk on top of it, and swing from bar to bar. The eight long, gray metal pipes are much larger than my hands, and I make my way across the horizontal ladder with only my hands, trying to see how many I can skip without falling.

Speaking of falling, it would have been a five- or six-foot drop to the asphalt. I had several of those experiences that resulted in a badly skinned knee or elbow, or at minimum a fresh red-colored scrape, or in the worst cases some blood running down my arm or leg. Those were the days! As Tarzan, a monkey, or a trapeze artist, I did my best to fly through the air. The freedom I felt and the fun I experienced on those bars are great memories. Today I play at ninja gyms and get to continue living so many of these fun experiences. If you are interested, I share much more about my personal ninja experience in both *The Heart of a Ninja* and *The Heart of a Ninja for Kids*.

How about you? Do you have a special place like this where you can be creative and do both risky and fun things, pushing yourself to see how far you can go? I hope you do. It was a good time with a lot of enjoyment and creativity.

Dipping Your Toe In

How close have you come to dipping your toe in the ninja warrior waters? Have you tried a ninja obstacle, or a full course run rather than just cheering on those fantastic competitors from the sideline or from your couch? When you do, I guarantee you will have more fun, experience encouragement, gain strength, and have more friends than you can imagine. You might come away with some aches, pains, a few injuries, and some disappointments, but you won't want to trade them for the world for the positive impacts ninja play will have on your life.

Through this book I hope to provide you with:
- A sense of how a ninja thinks and acts
- An awareness of 12 ninja traits that will help you improve your life
- Encouragement and hope for a more fun and better, healthy life

Bitten and Hooked

I'm convinced that as you read you will get hooked and want more. The next thing you know, you will be laughing more with new and exciting friends. One of these days you will look in the mirror and notice that you look different. It might be because of your increased strength, your improved balance, or your greater confidence in who you are. It might be due to what you can now do and who you are becoming. This is such a powerful experience. I hope you get hooked!

Free Gifts!

If you would like to receive any of the following free gifts, please request them at chriswarnky@gmail.com.

- A short video greeting from me with a bonus ninja training experience story
- A bonus story about my 2017 National Ninja League announcing experience

Let's dive into *Twelve Traits of a Ninja* and see how they can encourage and inspire you to have more fun and live a better life.

Chapter 1

Twelve Traits of a Ninja

What is in the heart of a ninja? What do we feel? How do we think? Do we all feel and think the same? If we have some common traits, what are they?

Ninja Traits

Based on my experience and exposure to hundreds of other ninjas, I believe there are many traits that most ninjas share. I have identified what I call 12 core traits of a ninja. I live or try to live each of these traits. What traits come to your mind? How many can you come up with? How well do these traits relate to helping you live your life? Are they just traits for a ninja course or obstacle?

I grouped these 12 traits into three categories: Obstacles, The Right Environment, and Study. Each has four individual traits.

Here are the ninja traits:

Obstacles

1. The desire to take on obstacles
2. The desire to stretch and see how much you can grow
3. It's you versus the obstacle, not others
4. The knowledge that every obstacle is different

The Right Environment

5. Encouragement, support, and celebration
6. Always playing: everything is a game
7. Growth and strength take time and work
8. Do it even in the midst of fear

Study

9. The desire to listen, study, and learn
10. Share of yourself and your knowledge
11. Explore your options
12. Failure is part of growing and getting stronger

How well do you apply or live these traits in your daily life? How would you rate yourself on a scale of one to five for each of them, five being "I am a model for others to follow" and one reflecting that you don't live that trait at all today?

Of these, which are your top three, the ones you live the best; and which are your bottom three, the ones that

need the most development? How would your life be different if you could improve your bottom three traits? I'm sure it could have a big impact on your life.

Adding a little structure to the way we look at and evaluate something can be so helpful. I hope you find the structure of these 12 traits to be helpful and motivational.

After reading about each of these traits I hope you decide to work to apply each of them in your life.

Let's take a look at the first category of traits, Obstacles.

Chapter 2

Obstacles – Traits 1 and 2

1. The Desire to Take on Obstacles

A Negative Image

What do you think if you hear someone talking about dealing with an obstacle? The word *obstacle* can have a negative image. It's something that gets in the way, a problem to face. Obstacles to living the way we want to live – "life obstacles" – are less visible than ninja obstacles. They can be complex, which can make them more difficult to solve. A life obstacle prevents us from moving forward. We must take on that obstacle and beat it to be able to move on. We can learn a lot from the ninja mindset, using ninja obstacles as examples of how we approach life.

I often want to avoid life obstacles. As an example, I don't like to update my business finances on a monthly basis. I don't do it often so I'm not very efficient when I do it. With my business I just want to have fun coaching people to a better life. I see the administrative part of my business as an obstacle that I have to do.

I need to better see my obstacles as things that must be addressed to move forward. Having the mind of a ninja can be helpful to me in identifying better ways to overcome them. I need to more consistently find ways to deal with them by playing with them and making them more fun.

Hunger

I enjoy watching ninjas approach obstacles. They hunger to face and take on an obstacle to see if they can beat it. They have a hunger to study how they and other ninjas have beaten it; a hunger for more information, or "beta" insights from people who test the obstacles; and a hunger to exchange ideas and approaches to find the best way to beat the obstacle.

It's fun to watch ninjas intensely observe testers as they go through an *ANW* course. I've been in Las Vegas when ninjas (I won't mention names) just happened to be walking by the course, which is surrounded by a chain-link fence and blocked by dark tarps to prevent outsiders from seeing the course. Some of them will get down on their hands and knees, or down on the ground like an alligator, to move along the fence below the black tarps, doing all they can to see how a tester is performing on the course. This doesn't usually last long before a security guard sees them and tells them to move along. (They might not look like ninjas, but I can identify them!) They want to observe all they can of someone else's attempts to beat the obstacles. They're hungry to learn more that could be helpful when they get their chance to run the course. Many ninjas who either were not invited to compete that year or did not qualify for the finals will pay their own traveling expenses for a chance to test an obstacle at the Las Vegas *ANW* venue.

How do you approach your life obstacles? Do you do it with the mind of a ninja? Do you know you can find a way to beat them? Do you hunger to prove yourself by taking on that obstacle? Can you apply the heart of a ninja to an obstacle you're facing? How could it be helpful and stimulating for you? It's a much better approach than feeling dread and being overwhelmed. It can be so powerful to say to yourself, "I can take on this obstacle and beat it," whatever it may be.

2. The Desire to Stretch and See How Much You Can Grow

How often do you stretch? (I don't mean physically, though physical stretching can also help.) How often do you try something new or try something in a different way than you have done it in the past? What are you doing to stretch and grow yourself? When was the last time you set a PR (personal record)?

Your PRs

A PR can be how fast you can finish your homework, how fast you can make a sandwich, how fast you can do five push-ups, or how many you can do. Gaining efficiency and strength can be very rewarding. I get excited every time I set and achieve a new PR because I've improved myself with a new skill or ability.

What PRs have you recently set? What PRs could you and would you like to set? What PRs would be most helpful to you? Consider creating some new goals and working to set new PRs. They're powerful tools for helping you stretch and grow. Each time you do, it provides a tremendous feeling of excitement.

Ninjas always look for new ways to take on an obstacle. They say, "I wonder if I could beat that obstacle if I changed my approach?" This perspective can apply to well over 100 obstacles in most ninja gyms: "I wonder if I could skip the second cannon ball and go for the third one. Would it help me get through the obstacle better or faster?" (A cannon ball is a large hanging ball; the challenge is in grabbing a sphere rather than something easier like a rope or a bar.) "I wonder if I could run down just the left side of the slanted steps," which is now done regularly by some of the top ninjas. Being open and flexible about new approaches is standard for a ninja.

Exploring Options

It's inspiring to hear a ninja say, "What if I two-step the warped wall rather than using three or four steps like most ninjas?" Or, "What if I quickly *match* (grab with both hands) on the rings rather than swing across with one hand on each ring?" The ideas that come to mind and are often attempted are so fun to see and try myself. The creativity is amazing!

Another example is on the quintuple steps – a version of the steps that has been the first obstacle on the show for many years and which you can see in ninja gyms around the country. These steps are set so that you jump back and forth, left and right, across multiple steps. During a practice time, ninja Dennis Lappin and others at the Classic City Center ninja course in Waterloo, Indiana, used their agility and speed to skip the second step altogether and instead run from the first to the third step, continuing along to the fourth and fifth steps to finally jump to the landing pad. By doing that they were able to trim their run times by a second or two by not jumping back and forth twice. It also provided them with more momentum to quickly leap to the landing pad.

It's a lot of fun to listen to ninjas talking about it and then see them experiment with their ideas to see if they can be successful. Planning for the most efficient approach is key for success. Sometimes our plans work... and sometimes they don't. Figuring out whether a new approach or technique provides an advantage is always on the mind of a ninja.

I Couldn't... Yet

I tried the skipping-the-second-step method, like Dennis and others had been doing, and I couldn't do it. To be successful I had to jump to my right and land with my left foot on the first step rather than the more natural outside or right foot. That was way too uncomfortable at that point in my development. I couldn't do it – yet – in the short time I had to prepare for the competition the next day. It's best to do what you find works best for you. A technique that works well for one ninja with their body type might not be the best approach for another. I've learned to listen to my body as I try to find approaches that work best. It's a process to learn and grow in these ways.

Working Up to It

In the past I have not been a very flexible guy. My legs are quite tight, so I do not yet have the stride and leg power of many of my younger fellow ninjas. This is a good example of getting to know my body, listening to it, and not pushing too hard too quickly, which can result in an injury. This doesn't mean that I don't push myself. It means that I'm cautious and careful when trying new things and that I might take a different approach based on what I've learned about my body at my age. I want to develop the ability to do many of these moves, but I must work up to them.

Do you want to stretch? The first step is to set some goals and strive to reach some new PRs. I encourage you to stretch and see what you can do that you have never done before.

Chapter 3

Obstacles – Traits 3 and 4

3. It's You versus the Obstacle, Not Others

Comparing Yourself to Others

How often do you compare yourself to others? How does comparing help you or hurt you? For many of us it causes negative feelings. We compare the greatest strength of others to our average strength or weakness. When we do that, it's easy to get discouraged.

I love the fact that most ninjas approach the sport with a "me versus the obstacle" mindset rather than "me versus someone else." You only control yourself, not others. If you want to improve what you control, focus on yourself and not on others. You can learn and grow from the experience of others without comparing your performance to theirs. This ninja trait has helped me realize how often I compare myself to others.

Focus on What You Control

When you focus on yourself and an obstacle instead of on how someone else tackles the obstacle, you have much better control of the results. You can study the obstacle and evaluate your abilities relative to it. An example from the ninja world is focusing on your balance skills, including your ability on rolling objects, wobbly objects, bouncy objects, and sinking or soft objects. When your focus is on the requirements of an obstacle and your skill level, you're truly productive. Your mind can evaluate your best options and how to best use those options.

Prioritize

All my ninja skills need improvement. When I train, I prioritize balance, core strength, and finger strength. I usually spend time on at least two balance obstacles. In addition, I often do what I call "knee-ups" to strengthen my core as I perform a dead hang or pull-up; I pull my knees up to the bar. I also do dead hangs on various obstacles, hanging by one or two hands from a bar, a rock-climbing hold, a ring, a peg, a cannon ball, or whatever. Building my skills in many areas positions me to beat many types of obstacles and allows me to have more fun and play longer on a course.

Focusing on the obstacles and your skill level is a more productive way to live and to compete in a ninja competition. It's so much more fulfilling than comparing yourself to others.

What skills are you developing? How much better prepared could you be to face life and ninja obstacles if you worked harder at developing additional skills?

4. The Knowledge that Every Obstacle Is Different

Are all obstacles in life and on ninja courses the same? Absolutely not! With ninja warrior you face both different obstacles and obstacles that are similar yet different in some way. There are some standard obstacles that appear on most every *ANW* city qualifier course. The first obstacle is always some type of steps and the warped wall is always the last obstacle. Over the years, even these obstacles have changed slightly, which has been enough to make them a lot harder for some ninjas. On city finals courses, the salmon ladder has always come after the warped wall.

Most of the other obstacles are different from course to course. Some are brand new and some are similar to obstacles used on other courses or in past years but with some new twist: a little farther apart, higher, having a greater tilt, a narrower or wider hold, a rope instead of a pole, rising instead of flat – you name it – something is going to be different, which adds to the challenge and excitement.

City Qualifier to Finals

Changes are also often made between the city qualifier round and the finals round. They might be the same obstacles, in the same order, but effectively the finals is a different course because some adjustments will have been made to at least a couple of the obstacles. Some of the first six obstacles cannot be approached the same way the second time. In addition, there are three to four additional obstacles added to the back of the course.

This is what makes *ANW* so different from other competitions and sports. Unlike baseball, football, basketball, tennis, volleyball, and all other sports, with ninja warrior the challenge is at least slightly different every time you compete. Those quick and efficient body adjustments you have to make in a split second can make all the difference in whether or not you have a successful ninja run.

What Would It Be Like?

What would it be like in football if on your first possession you had to gain 10 yards for a first down, and on your next possession you had to go 15 yards for a first down, and the field were only half as wide?

What would it be like to never be able to step on the ice before playing a hockey game? And to throw in a little ninja twist, this time the ice has a 5-percent uphill grade or slant from one end to the other, and the goal is half the usual size and faces sideways? And you must use a ping pong paddle and a softball instead of a hockey stick and puck. Now that would be a good version of ninja hockey.☺

Ninja warrior is different and challenging in unique ways. There is no practice on the actual obstacles. You hope your diverse training has prepared you for the exciting moment when you get to compete on those cool obstacles. Once you have started a run, if you misstep or misjudge a movement or lose your grip and fall, the fun is instantly over. Its "one and done." All you can do is reflect after the fact to optimize future runs. If you're on an obstacle before you're scheduled to compete, you're disqualified. It's just like life – surprises continually pop up all around us.

Training on Similar Obstacles

Most of the obstacles ninjas train on are different from those on an official *ANW* course. Local gyms don't have the funding of NBC, so they do their best to simulate obstacles on a much smaller budget.

Training on similar obstacles is still very helpful when it comes to developing skills and abilities, with the hope that your new skills will carry over to obstacles you might face at a local gym or on an *ANW* course. Each skill you develop is helpful when it comes time to adapt to the peculiarities of a course. Timing, confidence, technique, strength, and speed are beneficial as new obstacles are faced. Ninjas are constantly testing and trying different types of obstacles to improve their dynamic balance; core strength; quick, light foot movements; leg power for strides and hops; arm and grip strength; and overall agility and technique.

In addition to local ninja gym classes, open gyms, and *ANW* competitions, there are ninja leagues you can participate in. Three of the most popular currently are the World Ninja League (WNL), the Ultimate Ninja Athlete Association (UNAA), and The Federation of Ninja Athletics (FINA). I've participated in some of these competitions across the United States. Leagues give ninjas the opportunity to qualify at local competitions across the country for a national or world finals competition at the end of the season, competing against the best of the best. Many of the top ninjas from *ANW* participate in at least one of the leagues.

Ninjas develop skills so they can successfully face new obstacles. Through training and preparation, many skills become natural, creating muscle memory so that the ninja can focus on the subtle differences that happen in the moment and their body can make the necessary movements to complete an obstacle. One of the things I love about this sport is that it's a continual learning process and you never fully arrive. You can always learn to move more efficiently and gain endurance and power. The best part is that it feels so good to be strong in both my mind and body, helping me become the best version of myself.

Ninja Obstacles Are Like Life

Ninja obstacles can be a great analogy for life obstacles because both present a challenge we must face. In ninja competitions, the obstacles come back to back to back, and it's the same in life. We don't get to practice on the exact obstacles that we face on a ninja course or in life. We must find ways to successfully get through the challenges and we must live with the results of the choices we have made. Keeping ourselves healthy and having good thoughts enables us to face each of them. The lessons we learn from ninja training and competitions can help us in our daily lives.

How well do you prepare and train for obstacles in life? They can be different from what you have experienced in the past and they can occur back to back to back. What skills can you develop and what training can help you better prepare for overcoming life obstacles or challenges? I encourage you to develop the heart of a ninja and develop your skills so that when challenges come you're ready to take them on and beat them.

When it comes to planting a seed, the environment is so important. Rich soil allows an acorn to grow into a mighty oak tree. In poor soil that same acorn will dry out and decay or may even be eaten by a squirrel. A healthy environment is very important for our growth and for living a healthy life. In the next couple of chapters, we'll look at living in the right environment.

Chapter 4

The Right Environment – Traits 5 and 6

5. Encouragement, Support, and Celebration

Encouragement

Where do you turn in the good times and in the bad? Where do you get encouragement and support when you need it? Do you have a group that will be there for you? Some people turn to God. Some have a supportive family or group of friends. Some don't have anyone or anywhere to go to for encouragement and support... yet. How about you?

As ninjas, we are confident in our ninja community. We know the support we'll get. Ninjas like to grow, develop, push, and test themselves. We are there to support each other when we face obstacles or challenges. We thrive on exploring and expanding our boundaries, pushing past obstacles, and enjoying life to the fullest. The ninja community is so encouraging.

Support

I've been blessed to experience that level of support over and over. I've seen it at my daughter Michelle's gym, Movement Lab Ohio (MLAB OH), Classic City Ninja Warrior, The Edge, XT Fitness, and at other ninja gyms across the country. I've seen it at *ANW* city qualifying sites and at the Las Vegas *ANW* finals site! I've seen it at parks like the Scioto Audubon in Columbus, Ohio, and at Venice Beach in Los Angeles. Ninjas support and encourage each other in both their successes and failures. We relate well to each other.

Celebration

I love achieving a new PR when other ninjas are in the gym. I remember the excitement and celebration I experienced the first time I stuck an eight-foot lache. The high fives and hoots and hollers were so fun.

My ninja buddies had to remind me to celebrate the first time I made it across a difficult narrow ledge – a longer-reach cliff-hanger obstacle. I was so focused on my technique that I didn't realize it was the first time I had cleared it. As always, celebration, high fives, and hugs followed.

And I remember the support I got at an MLAB OH ninja competition when I fell on the third obstacle, a balance tank (PVC pipe) obstacle. I felt badly about going down early on an obstacle that I had trained for but couldn't beat that day. To lift my spirits, I immediately received many hugs, high fives, and words of encouragement to keep at it and keep learning from each experience.

Vulnerability

We all can relate to experiencing both success and failure. Wouldn't it be amazing if you had this level of support from everyone you know? Ninjas put themselves out there, revealing their fears when taking on obstacles. It's scary to share our fears, but that's what it takes to be part of the ninja community. You and the obstacle are on full display for fellow ninjas and instructors. This sharing opens the door for the support we all want and need.

Where do you need to be more open and share the challenges you're facing so that you can get the support you need? Sharing fears is a key trait that the ninja environment provides. We can learn so much from sharing our concerns and fears. I encourage you to take that step to open that door for more support. The power it can provide is amazing.

6. Always Playing: Everything Is a Game

How much of your day includes play? How often do you make what you have to do a game, to see if you can do it better or faster than the last time? What if that was how you approached life on a regular basis? How could that improve your life?

Make It into a Game

My dad used to occasionally cut our backyard grass in a curvy maze for us kids to play on. As an adult and homeowner, I now know why it was the backyard and not the front; I'm sure the neighbors appreciated a nicer-looking, well-cut front yard. It was so much fun to run through the maze, jumping across the cut areas and sometimes playing tag where everyone had to stay in the cut area while they were

being chased. That is a lifetime memory and one that shows how the simplest situation can be made into a game. That experience as a kid probably led to why I created Ninja Balance Obstacle Tag, which we sometimes play at MLAB OH during open gyms.

How are you turning your responsibilities into games or opportunities to play? If you're not, you should!

One of the tips I learned from one of the John Maxwell Team faculty members was to set a timer when I have to get something done. The task then becomes a game as I focus on what is in front of me, trying to beat the clock to complete the task and win the little time game I just created. It can be as simple as going through my emails and responding to them within 15 minutes, which sometimes can be a real push and a race against the clock.

Sometimes I find it best to bundle two or three activities together and give myself a time to complete all of them. It could be organizing the things I need to do for the day, calling someone, or outlining and writing a first draft of a writing assignment. I might give myself 35 minutes to complete these tasks, which is achievable if I stay focused. It becomes a game. Can I win? It's so much fun to beat that clock!

Using a timer helps me focus, and when I don't beat my time, I just reset the clock and start again, staying on my mission to see if I can get it done before my next alarm. I turn these activities into a game instead of just following through on a bunch of things I must do. It enables me to have fun, stay motivated, and focus on the things that are most important.

Ninjas Love to Play

Ninjas play a lot and have a lot of fun when they have access to just about any space or object on this planet, especially if they're around other ninjas. It can be in the hallway or bathroom of a building, in the entrance to a store, or on the steps to a school or church. It seems that any and every space is a place to see if we can do something new or do something better than we have before. I have adopted that orientation as well. I may not always take action on my thoughts, but boy do I have the thoughts! "I wonder if I could..."

After an Ohio State University Buckeye basketball game, Carolyn and I were walking through the narrow, painted-cement-block hallway from inside the arena to the concession stand area. The hallway is wide enough for two people to pass comfortably or three to pass tightly. I couldn't help it. I saw that hallway as a ninja spider-jump opportunity. I said to Carolyn, "I think I can stick this." I meant jumping up in the air, kicking my feet out, and sticking one foot on each side of the hallway, suspending my body in the air. I would not have tried it if the walls were drywall; I know that could have turned out badly, with a big hole in the wall.

With a grin I looked to Carolyn to see how she would react. She responded with, "Really? Are you sure you can do it and not hurt yourself?" I wasn't warmed up, I was wearing jeans, and I had on old tennis shoes, but I said, "I think I can."

I checked behind me to make sure no one was coming; I handed her my empty souvenir Buckeye cup; and here we go. With a swing of my arms and hands, I leaped into the air and kicked out my feet and... not quite. I slid down the concrete blocks. Okay, one more time, here we go. I swung my arms down and back and then up into the air in front of me, and pop, my feet kicked out, and... sure enough, my shoes stuck to the walls! This brought a gigantic smile to my face, ear to ear. My shoes were clean, so no marks were left on the wall. I checked.

It's so much fun to try something I've not done and make it, or at least come close. When I miss, I think, "What could I have done differently?" In this case, "I stuck it! I won!" on my second attempt.

Play Some More

I believe life is better when we include some time to play – and maybe a bunch of it. When we turn boring activities into games, they become enjoyable opportunities to challenge ourselves. It's play when we enjoy growing or performing beyond what we have done before. It can be something physically challenging or just doing something with our minds.

This play shows up especially at a ninja gym. Many gym owners open their gyms the night before a competition so ninjas can come in and play. They get to see what they can jump to and from, run across, swing from, bounce to and from, push off from, or any number of other moves. The next day, after the exertion and play of the night

before, they line up to compete on the official ninja course. A competition can take anywhere from five to 12 hours.

What happens immediately after a competition? There is often another one, two, three, or even four hours of ninjas just hanging around playing and trying obstacles. Now that they have seen their peers take on obstacles in their own unique ways, there are new approaches and ways to try to beat the obstacles. They're hungry to get back out there and try more options. This time is called "redemption time," when you get to try again to beat an obstacle that took you down during the formal competition. Ninjas often try to see who can do the most of some new, unique thing. Who can last the longest on a dead hang? Who can do the most pull-ups? Who can bounce the highest on a trampoline (tramp) and grab and hold the highest obstacle? Who can... you name it. It's about play and challenging ourselves to achieve more than we have before. It's like one big round of King of the Hill.

Are you playing? What new ideas came to mind as you read my examples above? What can play look like for you? I'm convinced there are limitless options for adding fun to our routine lives through adding the idea of playing.

Life is so much better when you're encouraged and supported and when you include play in your life.

Next, we'll see how important it is to stay with it when you're working to accomplish something, and also how to face your fears.

Chapter 5

The Right Environment – Traits 7 and 8

7. Growth and Strength Take Time and Work

When you're working on an assignment or goal, how quickly do you expect to see progress? Your goal might be developing a totally new skill like playing the piano (a middle-school experience for me); riding a unicycle (I also learned to do that in middle school); speaking a new language (like my attempts at Russian when Michelle was working in Kazakhstan); riding a two-wheeled wave board (which I learned in my fifties); being able to give engaging, powerful speeches (which I learned in my late fifties); or any number of other goals. You might want to bench press a certain weight, run a mile in a certain amount of time, or beat a particular computer game.

Growth and significant progress do not usually come quickly. In most cases making significant progress or developing a new skill or strength takes a long time of continual effort and practice. In most cases we have to achieve many small, even what might feel like tiny improvements over time, before we feel we have really made significant progress.

Repeated Effort

Ninjas know that it takes time and repeated effort to achieve a new milestone on an obstacle or course. That's why they spend hour after hour, day after day focused on the same small skill until they achieve the improvement they want. Ninjas Noel Reyes and Bryce LaRoche shared with me that it took a long time to master a slack line. Now it's amazing to watch them walk or do tricks on one. They make it look effortless because they dedicated significant time, focus, and effort to develop that balance skill and the muscles required to be on a slack line.

I could share many personal examples of my putting in that kind of time and effort. Probably the best example is the year and a half I worked on getting to the top of a 14-foot warped wall. That's running up the wall, grabbing the top, and pulling my chest above the top of the wall. At MLAB OH the ceiling interferes with standing on the top, so pulling my chest above the top was my goal to prove I had the strength to be able to stand on top.

Two Hours... A Little Perspective

Michelle was able to reach and catch the top of the 14-foot warped wall at Movement Lab New Jersey the first weekend she went there! That wall is one of the steepest in the country. She worked specifically on wall attempts for over two hours before she was able to stick it for the first time. Many guys use a three-step approach to run up the wall, which she tried. Then she tried a four-step approach and almost caught the top. After changing to the four-step approach she soon caught the top. She is just five feet four inches tall. Your height makes a big difference. I don't know how many times she attempted the wall during that two-hour period, but if she attempted it three or four times every five minutes, she probably made 30 or 40 attempts an hour. I can guarantee you that each attempt drains you of energy and makes the next attempt that much harder. I need a good breather between attempts. Michelle stuck with it until she reached her goal!

I was 57 when I first attempted to catch the top of a 14-foot warped wall. I spent more than 18 months and made over 1,000 attempts before I was able to reach and hold on to the top for the first time. I made at least 15 attempts most weeks for 18 months. I stayed focused and continually worked on my strength, technique, and mindset, which are all so critical. That was a lot of work for a 57/58-year-old. It was crazy to look back at a video of my first attempt on the wall; after finally being able to get to the top, my first attempt looked like I was trying to *walk* up to the top of the wall. I guarantee that on my first attempt I truly did give it all that I had at the time. I just did not have much to give when I first started. It felt so good to see the progress that I have been able to make.

I finally reached that milestone in early 2016, just days before my 59th birthday. I had set a goal of reaching it before I turned 59. Mission accomplished! Growth like that takes time and a lot of work.

Take the Hill

I now call the warped wall "a hill." I just keep running up the hill until I get to the top. When you first see a warped wall in person, standing on the floor and looking all the way to the top, I believe many see it as a tall, hard, nearly straight up monster of a brick wall that is nearly impossible to climb, be it 12 feet, 14 feet, or higher. Seeing it as a hill that I'm running up instead of a wall that I'm running into helps me more easily visualize being able to make it to the top.

Some of the guys at our gym can run up that wall with such power that they go for touching the building ceiling above the top of the wall, which is probably another three feet higher. This makes their top reach more like 17 feet. My focus continues to be on getting better at consistently catching the top of the 14-foot wall.

The warped wall is just one of over 100 skills I've been working on to slowly, consistently, and gradually make progress. Some of the other skills are leg strides, trampoline jumps, ring swings, pegboard moves, laches, and hops (a forward hop up with both feet).

These are examples of applying *yet* in my life. The key is celebrating my tiny improvements on each of these skills.

Pay the Price

Where are you frustrated with your progress? Where are you giving up when you should be pushing through? How much longer should you work at achieving your goal to persevere and stay with it? How long is just too long?

Progress and significant improvement require time and hard work, and a ninja is willing to pay that price. How about you? Are you willing to pay that price to gain that prize you have been working for? I hope you are.

Growth and progress feel so good and can create many new opportunities for us. They give us hope and energy, which spill into the other areas of our lives. You can grow and become so much more than you are today. I know you can!

8. Do It Even in the Midst of Fear

Where and when do you face fear? (We all do!) What fear is shutting you down or holding you back from achieving something that is important to you or could have a powerful impact on your life? Fear is a tremendously powerful issue for all of us. The more we learn to face it, embrace it, and overcome it, the better our lives become on all fronts.

Ninja warrior is about facing your fears and overcoming them. From the day I stepped on my first ninja obstacle – the quad steps on a late Saturday night at the end of one of Michelle's ninja competitions – to this day, I've been learning to better face fears, head on. I'm now bolder when facing many of my fears, though there are still those that can at times shut me down.

Baby Steps

I've found that taking baby steps toward facing my fears is one of my best strategies. These include taking on my first attempt at an eight-foot lache, the quad steps, a salmon ladder, and so many others.

When under-five-feet-tall ninja Peggy Hale couldn't yet catch a 10-foot-high bar from a mini-tramp, she used baby steps. She started by moving the tramp closer to the bar. As she experienced consistent success, she pulled the tramp back another five inches. She continued pulling the tramp farther back and she nailed it repeatedly, pulling the tramp back by baby steps until she had reached her maximum skill level for that day. It was a lot of fun to watch Peggy nail it from a much greater distance by first experiencing success from a short distance. She used baby steps.

In my first attempts on a salmon ladder I started by simply jerking the bar up off of the rung, and then jerking it up to the bottom of the next rung. I was able to practice the jerk move without having to focus on the pull out, reach up, and placement of the bar on the next rung. It's amazing how helpful these baby steps can be in learning how to beat an obstacle, or the first step of an obstacle.

What fears do you face? Whether it's meeting new people, having a hard conversation with someone, learning a new subject, learning a new phone or computer – you name it, fear is common in all of us. What baby steps can you take to help you move forward so you don't have to take on the whole challenge all at once? How can baby steps help you experience some success and move you closer to facing your fear and addressing your challenge? Taking baby steps is a great strategy.

F.E.A.R.

Fear has been described as False Expectations Appearing Real – F.E.A.R. For many of us that's a pretty good description of fear. How true is this statement for you: I've experienced many horrible things in my life... most of which never happened (my version of a quote often mistakenly attributed to Mark Twain)? When we imagine the worst, our mind takes us through that experience as though we were living it, which can cause us worry and make us freeze in our tracks. When we visualize a situation ending in a good way, we gain the benefit of hopeful thinking even if it doesn't fully turn out that way.

I have found that by breaking my fears down into baby steps on ninja courses – little successes – I can face more fears than I have in the past. I have learned that many of my fears truly are just fears, that they are not real, and that they are just False Expectations Appearing Real. I can do more than I thought I could. Working with baby steps on a ninja course has helped me improve other parts of my life as well. Another example is the fear I had about embarking on writing books. By taking one step at a time I'm now an author of five books and more are coming! I did it (with the encouragement and support of many others, as you'll see in the next chapter)!

What fears are holding you back? How can you better face them? What are some baby steps you can take? It feels so good inside when you're able to overcome a challenge. How could a gym or a ninja course be helpful to you in this way? It's an excellent place to practice overcoming fears. Why not give it a try? I'm convinced it can really help, and at a minimum you will experience something new, which is always exciting!

What type of environment do you live in? Being in a positive, encouraging environment makes a big difference in our lives. To be healthy and strong you need to be patient as you work at learning or accomplishing something, and you need to make sure you're not allowing fear to shut you down.

We're forced to study and learn when in school. In the next chapter we'll see how ninjas love to study and learn.

Chapter 6

Study – Traits 9 and 10

9. The Desire to Listen, Study, and Learn

Do you listen to, study, and learn from others when you're facing a tough challenge? Do you say, "I've got this"? There are so many things we can accomplish when we watch and learn from others.

Open Gym Times

Many gyms are open for two to four hours the night before a competition or immediately following a competition. The night before is a time for ninjas to study the gym and play on the obstacles even though they will not see the actual obstacle setup for the competition. These are fun nights, and in many ways even more valuable to me than the actual competitions.

I love these open gym times because I get to see how ninjas approach an obstacle I've never seen or one that's set up differently than I've seen. There is so much to learn just by watching.

The buzz around the gym on these evenings is "What do you think will be used for the course tomorrow?" "What modifications will they make to the obstacles we see now?" "Will they eliminate a hold or a rope or extend the distance?" "What might they add that isn't currently set up?" "What have you heard that might surface in the morning at the comp?"

The buzz and evaluation are constant. We study how each obstacle is approached by each ninja, trying to figure out the best approach for us. "Can I reach the way he reached?" "Do I have the same finger strength or 90-degree hold strength that she has?" "Can his method work for me?" "What step, hold, or rope did she skip, and how did he accomplish that?" A lot of that study takes place the night before so that the ninja is ready to face the course the next day. The goal is to use everything you have learned in training in the weeks and months beforehand so you can be more efficient and effective in facing the obstacles back to back during a competition.

My Book-Writing Obstacle

The book-writing process, which I could look at as an obstacle, was something I had never done before. I could have just started writing and figured it out as I went, or observed, listened to, and learned from many others. I decided I could do it better and faster with the help of others who had already written books – those who were ahead of me.

I read three books on the book-writing process and then I joined a helpful group of writers. As they were writing their books, I asked questions, listened to, and learned from them, to help me take on my book-writing obstacle. I approached the process much differently than I would have if I had tried to do it on my own. And I was much more efficient and effective than I would have been without the help of these others.

I encourage you to listen to others and their ideas and learn from their experiences so you can be more effective in beating your obstacles. This way is so much better than taking the hard road by yourself.

Study is such an important element of growth. Could you be a better, stronger person if study were a bigger part of your life? What would change for you? We are not like trees that just need soil, sunlight, and water to grow. We have to be intentional. Make study a key part of your life.

10. Share of Yourself and Your Knowledge

Do you share what you know to help others? Do you give of yourself to help family, friends, or people you don't even know? The heart of a ninja is to provide encouragement and support to others and to also enjoy receiving it.

It's so much fun to help someone with something they're trying for the first time. It's rewarding to help someone go where they've never been. Most of us get excited when we achieve something new.

Sharing Tips

In my ninja experience there has been a lot of sharing. The lache tips I received at MLAB OH from Jesse Wildman, Kyle Wheeler, and Josh Wallis were helpful. I remember getting tips from ninja and gym owner Glenn Davis during the recording of *ANW* "All-Stars" in 2015. He shared with me various ways to grab a bar when swinging and lacheing. I'm reminded of tips I received from Jesse Labreck on how to make a move on the BOSU® ball at the Rockford ninja warrior course. (A BOSU is a soft, two-foot-wide, half-round ball that tests your balance. The name BOSU comes from BOth Sides Up.) I appreciate the cannon-ball-swinging tips I received from ninja Sean Darling-

Hammond, and the slack-line tips from Josh Wallis, Sean Noel, Noel Reyes, Bryce LeRoche, and others. I value the razor's-edge tips that a top ninja shared with me after my 2017 run on the *ANW* city qualifier course. (I share much more about that in *What Just Happened?: The Run*, the story of my 2017 *ANW* course run in Cleveland.) I could go on and on with so many examples.

Each of these ninjas wanted to help me get better at what I was trying to achieve. Often the advice is offered when I'm either attempting an obstacle or studying it. Other times I ask, and the help is provided.

There is a wrong time to ask: just before a ninja is scheduled to run in a competition, or when they're already in a conversation with someone else. It's common sense not to interrupt when someone is focused on what they're doing. I hope I'm getting better at asking only at good times. I know there have been times when I realized, after the fact, that I was making a comment or asking a question when someone was preparing to run the course, so now I'm careful to be sure I'm not interrupting their train of thought. And if you've asked and asked for advice and taken a lot of someone's time, let them get back to their own training. This is a very sharing community, and it goes both ways. Ninjas help each other and discuss approaches to obstacles all the time.

I also love being at MLAB OH and helping first-timers or less experienced ninjas with a skill or tip that I've learned. It's so much fun to see them achieve a new level of success because of something I was able to share with them.

Where Could You Be Sharing?

What do you know that could be helpful to others? Who could you encourage if you were to share with them something you know?

The key is to be sure that the person would like to hear what you would like to share. We've all experienced being told something by a know-it-all. It's difficult to listen in those times, and much easier when it comes from someone who we know cares about us. The best approach is to ask the question "Would you like to hear my thoughts on how you could better do that?"

Ask for Help

The right insight or information can save you seconds (very important on a ninja course), minutes, hours, days, weeks, or even months or years. It takes both humility and boldness to ask someone for help. It can be scary to ask, but keep in mind that most people like to help, and if you don't ask you're taking away the opportunity for them to get to help. The heart of a ninja is to both share and receive a lot of help. When we listen, study, and learn, and when we share what we know with others, we become stronger. How can you learn and better apply these ninja traits?

In the next chapter I share how important it is to explore options when you're facing an obstacle, and how important it is to learn to deal with failures. We all face them.

Chapter 7

Study –
Traits 11 and 12,
and a Summary

11. Explore Your Options

When you run into a problem or obstacle, how many options do you usually consider? Often it seems we only identify one or two. Many of us don't take the time to look at an obstacle from different angles, which can prevent us from seeing other ways to address it. We feel trapped and limited in how to face it. When we dread using the only option that comes to mind, we try to avoid the obstacle altogether, which can make things even worse.

When it comes to beating ninja obstacles, it's eye-opening to watch the top ninjas. What appears to be a standard way to take on an obstacle is usually different from the way top ninjas do it. Yes, there's a big gap between my skills and theirs, but there's also a gap between the way I think about and approach an obstacle and how they do it.

I'm trying to consistently take the time in advance to think of at least three or four ways that I could approach an obstacle.

Ninja Options

I was competing in a mini competition at MLAB OH. One of the early obstacles was a series of slanted steps set up in a unique way. There were seven slanted steps that formed an L shape.

I smoothly made it through the steps using a few single steps and a few triple steps. A little later one of the top ninjas who won the second competition that night – "The Ninja Mailman," Cory Cook – went through the same obstacle. He skipped one of the steps on the right because he noticed that the last three steps on the left were set much like a ninja sonic curve, for which you single-step the steps as you round the curve to the end of the obstacle. This move feels more natural and it's a faster way to move through them. This technique could have saved me energy and two seconds or so on my run time. If you can save two or three seconds at five points along a course it can reduce your time by 10 to 15 seconds, which can move you up the finish placement by several spots. That is significant in a competition.

Moving through a course with speed and efficiency is what wins competitions. Although ninjas always root for everyone to do their best, we want to do our best as well.

When Carolyn and I were in the stands in 2015 at the first *Team Ninja Warrior* competition in Los Angeles, it was exciting to watch those talented ninjas go head-to-head focusing on efficiency and speed. The fifth obstacle in that course was a set of two rings that you used to move along several pegs up and down a long inverted, V-shaped structure. It was very interesting to see ninjas use various techniques to move across them as fast as they could. Some directly faced the peg and structure, a few had the strength and reach to skip a peg, and others used the rings more like monkey bars, swinging one hand down and under their body to swing forward to the next peg.

Then, a very talented ninja, was in a head-to-head match-up on the course. He was slightly behind when he got to the rings-and-pegs obstacle. When he got to the back third of that obstacle he made one of his routine powerful swings backward, and the next thing we knew he was flying forward through the air toward the landing platform and past the other ninja. He skipped two pegs and flew forward over 15 feet – or rather SOARED! That move immediately put him in the lead and sent a chill of excitement through the entire crowd. To see him soar that far through the air was amazing! No previous competitor had attempted that move and taken that risk. He was the first. Soon others used the same technique, or at least tried it. Some were successful and some were not.

He thought it through, considered his options, and with his incredible strength and body awareness made a fantastic move that saved him energy for the end of the course. It also saved him valuable time and gave the crowd a tremendous experience to enjoy and savor.

Unlimited Options

Our options are almost unlimited if we take the time to think before we act. With preparation and dedication to developing body awareness, the most experienced ninjas can make adjustments in a split second. Sometimes what we envision will work goes wrong in the moment, and quick changes are required. Additional options on a course can include skipping a rung, step, or knob; single-stepping something instead of using multiple steps; reducing the number of steps used; building your swing before making a transition; using the swing of your body to assist you through a series of hand obstacles rather than using only your strength; using your feet on a rope or an I-beam to save your arm strength; leaning forward as you approach a warped wall; and so many others.

Great ninjas consider many options before taking on an obstacle. They leverage their abilities to maximize their performance. They use the options that will work best for them based on their current strengths and weaknesses.

How many options do you consider when you face a problem or obstacle? Do you consider your strengths and weaknesses? Sometimes it's hard to take the extra time, but it's worth every minute.

12. Failure Is Part of Growing and Getting Stronger

How does failure fit into your life and growth? If it does, does it move you toward growth and a greater commitment to learn, or does it shut you down and send you into discouragement or depression?

Ninjas know that failure is a part of the process. Ninja courses and competitions are about learning to deal with disappointment, both on *ANW* and in local ninja competitions. Very few competitors successfully finish a course, and even when they do, it is rarely on the first try.

ANW City Qualifier Disappointment

One hundred to 110 ninjas typically get to compete on a city qualifier course. Of those, only 30 percent or less qualify for the finals. That means that 70 or more competitors will no longer be competing that season. That can create a lot of disappointment, and those ninjas whose season has ended abruptly could consider it a failure. This feeling of disappointment can be quite strong, especially considering the years of training and preparation they have invested. "I could have" and "I should have" conversations can dominate the thoughts of those who fall earlier than they had hoped, which is most ninjas. The best way to use these thoughts and feelings is as motivation for more training.

ANW City Finals Disappointment

Of the 30 or so ninjas who move on to the city finals, only the top 12 (potentially a couple more based on the "women competitors" rule that was put in place in *ANW 9*) move on to the "Las Vegas Finals." Any ninja who finishes the city finals course gets invited to compete in Las Vegas, but that's usually far fewer than 12 ninjas. So over half of the competitors are likely to be very disappointed. *ANW* is about striving to succeed and learning how to deal with disappointment and failure.

Local Ninja Gym Competition Disappointment

Even at local ninja gym and ninja league competitions, with between 40 and a few hundred competitors, sometimes only one ninja finishes the course, or only a few finish a speed-based course, potentially five to 10 people. That is still at least a 70 percent or more failure or disappointment rate. This sport requires you to learn to deal with disappointment.

How do I respond when I've failed on an obstacle? Do I get frustrated and yell at the obstacle? Do I blame the balance beam, the bar I swung from, or the step I slid off? Do I make excuses? Do I think, "I can't do this!"? Do I say, "I hate this stupid course!"? No. At least not for long. I respond like other ninjas. I say, "I can't believe I just did that. I should have... stepped out farther, reached higher, skipped that step, or whatever to make it through that obstacle," and then I get a very strong urge to get right back on that obstacle and try it again with a better approach. I think about my performance, watch a video of my run, and study what I did and didn't do well. I get tips from fellow ninjas, and then I get back to work trying to beat that obstacle.

When I get home, I do what I can to duplicate the obstacle that took me out. I also set one up at the gym. I want to practice and practice until I'm able to beat that obstacle that took me down. I know with a little more preparation and focus I can beat the obstacle the next time I face it. And through my training I gain confidence in my abilities.

BOSU Step-Down

One example is when I went down on a BOSU-ball transition step-down to a snake bridge in a Rockford ninja competition. I studied that obstacle and tried to figure out how to better approach it.

At home I have a BOSU ball in the basement, so I brought it upstairs and set it on our dining room floor where there is a step down to our family room. It's only a six-inch step down, but when you add the height of the BOSU ball, it's a 13-inch drop, which was a good distance to practice. I practiced by bending one knee and extending the other foot in front and down the step to our family room floor.

As with my other obstacle experiences, my first few attempts were quite hard and not very successful. But the more attempts I made with each foot, the better I got at making that step. (I was tempted to use the word *easier*, but that's probably an overstatement of my skill; it is still a challenging move.) I also set up a similar obstacle in our garage and practiced the move there. And I set up the BOSU ball in the basement as part of a mini course with several balance obstacles. In that setup I moved to the BOSU ball from a teeter-totter and then had to step down onto a large PVC pipe that rolls along the floor, a version of what many ninjas call a balance tank.

I set up a similar BOSU-ball obstacle at MLAB OH during an open gym. I was stepping down from a vault box that held the BOSU ball, making it a much farther step down to a handrail-like balance obstacle. This was a much tougher challenge than just stepping down to the floor.

When an obstacle beats us, we want to work hard on that skill to ensure to the best of our ability that the same obstacle will not take us out in the same way again.

Baby's First Steps

One of the best examples of this is how we support a baby when they attempt to take their first step. We don't yell at them for falling or failing. We don't tell them to give up or to believe they will never walk. Instead we celebrate every move they make toward taking that first step. We cheer them on. We help them in every way possible both physically and with our words.

Failure is a part of our learning process. We all need a community to encourage and support us when we fail, and the ninja community is an ideal family as we move through failure to success.

I do my best to live this way. I take time to think about my experiences so I can learn from my failures. I don't want to experience failure in the same way with the same result a second time. I'm not perfect in this area, but I've made great improvements.

Thinking about and learning from our experiences is so powerful for our lives. For years I have prioritized setting aside time for reflection about my life. (And sometime down the road I will share my process and my thoughts about this reflection time in a future book.)

How much better off would you be if you saw your failures in this positive way? It can make your life better. Where do you need to apply this type of thinking that failure is a part of growing and getting stronger?

Twelve Traits Summary

You have now read about each of the 12 traits of a ninja, grouped by obstacles, right environment, and study. These aren't just traits for ninjas. They can help all of us.

I continue to work at better living each of them. I am most challenged by number 8, doing it in the midst of fear, and number 12, failure is part of growing and getting stronger.

Especially since suffering a concussion in early 2018 (another potential future book), I find that moving forward in the midst of fear is extra hard. On a ninja course I'm so much better when I only have to reach or step for my next move. My fear rises when I must throw my body forward and catch something or land on a platform a good distance away. I'm still hesitant. It's so frustrating, and yet I fully understand why. When you have had a serious injury it can absolutely fight to take over your mind and shut you down. Being cautious is very important, but I've been overly cautious since the incident. My best strategy continues to be taking progressive baby steps forward and slowly building up my confidence again to go in the midst of fear.

Failure has shut so many people down and caused them to give up. At times I can also live in this camp. Most recently I've had a series of hamstring pulls – four in slightly different places on the same leg within a three-month period. It can be so frustrating to have to sit on the sideline and rest and do my physical therapy exercises at a consistent, healthy pace. I want to be out there playing again, but I need to be patient and slowly get back to my normal, active, ninja self. My strategies have been staying lightly active, enjoying the experiences of my fellow ninjas (and not being jealous of their successes and growth), and listening well to their encouragement to stay with it and be patient. I continue to work on both of these traits in particular.

As you read through this summary, which one or two traits do you most need to develop to improve your life?

Obstacles

1. The desire to take on obstacles
2. The desire to stretch and see how much you can grow
3. It's you versus the obstacle, not others
4. The knowledge that every obstacle is different

The Right Environment

5. Encouragement, support, and celebration
6. Always playing: everything is a game
7. Growth and strength take time and work
8. Do it even in the midst of fear

Study

9. The desire to listen, study, and learn
10. Share of yourself and your knowledge
11. Explore your options
12. Failure is part of growing and getting stronger

I hope you're developing the heart of a ninja and that you're already developing many of these traits in your life. I hope you find them helpful.

What are your next steps relative to applying these ninja traits to your life? In the next chapter I share some tips I hope you find helpful.

Chapter 8

You, Too, Can Train as a Ninja Warrior

I Won

Over the past few years I've developed the heart of a ninja. It has been an unbelievable experience. I won, and so can you by playing and moving, training as a ninja. I've been a typical non-athlete. If I can do this and love it, learn and grow, and have more fun and energy, you can too.

All of us enjoy experiencing forward progress. You can improve your life, which will also positively impact your friends and family. It will make a difference. You matter!

Hopefully you have already made some positive changes based on what I've shared to encourage and challenge your heart and mind. I hope you will make even more changes in your life as you think about the key points in *Twelve Traits of a Ninja*. Improvements you make in yourself benefit you for the rest of your life.

Your Next Steps

What would be an appropriate next step forward for you right now? There are so many things you can do to add movement and play to your life. Here are a few ideas:

Google Searches

Use Google (or any other browser) to explore ninja warrior on the internet. I list some good Google search options in the "Ninja Resources" section at the back of this book. There are also many helpful ninja-related YouTube videos.

At Home

- Start skipping a step when you climb steps at home. Start by skipping one step each time. Then see if you can skip more than one. Finally, skip steps all the way to the top, or really push it and try skipping two steps. Make it a game. Set your own PRs to incorporate movement and play.
- Walk around the block. To turn it into a game, time yourself for a specific distance, trying to continually reduce your time; or set a time limit and see how far you can walk in that time, constantly trying to set a new PR – a greater distance traveled within that time. Can you get to an additional mailbox or a few feet farther each time?
- See how many steps it takes you to travel a distance – maybe 20 feet or five sections of a sidewalk. Try to reduce the number of steps you have to take. How long of a stride can you use and still

maintain your balance? Set a PR and improve on it. Have fun beating your own record.

- See how long or how far you can skip. It's a fun, playful, and freeing motion. Just doing it will bring a smile to your face. You can do it on a sidewalk, at the edge of a street, or in a parking lot. I usually try to do this either with others at a gym or when no one is around. That might apply for many of these fun suggestions.

At School

- See how many steps you can skip or how few steps you can take to the next floor or floors. Try doing it with no hands. You can even time yourself to see how fast you can do it.
- Stretch while you're sitting or standing. How long can you hold it?
- See how long you can balance on one foot.
- While standing on one leg, how many times can you bend over and touch the floor or something close to the floor? Remember, you have to do it with each leg. One may be a lot stronger than the other.

At a Park

- Climb up to and hang from the top support bar of a swing set or from a tree branch. How long can you hang? These are referred to as dead hangs. Try a pull-up, and if you're ambitious, try shaking out, which is when you hang by one hand and let the other arm dangle while you shake it out. The first time you do this will give you a quick sense of just how hard it is. It will help you appreciate what other ninjas can do.
- Balance on one of those concrete parking barriers at the front of a parking space. (Use one that does not have a car parked in front of it!☺) How long can you stay on? If you really want to have fun, try stepping across them from one parking spot to another. Those can be quite long strides and they're fun to try.

At a Ninja Gym

- Find out when a local ninja competition is taking place and go watch it.
- If you're within traveling distance of Columbus, Ohio, enroll in a Ninja Lite class at MLAB OH and learn from me as your instructor. I focus on safety, fun, and beginner ninja skills, in that order!

- Go to an open gym time at a ninja gym and start with a few simple obstacles.
- Enter a local competition. Many gyms offer various levels of competition. You don't have to start at the pro level. Enter the amateur, basic, or lowest level of competition. MLAB OH even offers mini-comps for just a few dollars and a few hours – not a full-scale, all-day event.

I hope these ideas open your mind to the unlimited number of ways you can include movement and play in your life, wherever you are. You can do it, and it will be good for you.

Thank you!

You've finished *Twelve Traits of a Ninja*. Thank you for joining me on this journey. I hope you enjoyed the experience and that you've learned some things that will help you. There are additional ninja resources in the remaining pages.

Share This Book with Others

Pass *Twelve Traits of a Ninja* on to someone you think would really enjoy it. You might want to recommend it to others or buy a copy for them as a gift. *Twelve Traits of a Ninja* is a great birthday gift! If you would like others to know how much you enjoyed the book, provide a review at Amazon.com.

Thanks for investing in yourself by reading this book. It will pay off for you. It's play time! Now get out there and live like a ninja!

Make it another great day, week, month, and year.
Your ninja, friend, author, coach, and *ANW* fan,
Chris Warnky

Ninja Resources

Ninja Gyms

Most gyms provide classes, open gym times, and competitions.

Movement Lab Ohio: http://www.mlabohio.com
       email: Info@mlabohio.com

Movement Lab (New Jersey): http://www.mlabnj.com

Movement Lab (Los Angeles): http://www.mlabca.com

There are many new gyms opening all the time.

Google Searches (content changes all the time)

- Ninja
- Ninja warrior
- Ninja gyms
- Ninja training
- Ninja camps
- Ninja leagues
- Parkour gyms
- Wolfpack tour

Equipment and Shoe Vendor Options

- 3Ball Climbing – cannon balls, etc.
- Atomik – cannon balls, etc.
- New Balance Shoes – Fresh Foam Zante (I use these for all my training. They're my favorites, with unbelievable traction for warped walls, spider-climbs, etc.)

American Ninja Warrior News Site

- ANWNation.com

Learn More

Contact Information

Chris Warnky, author, ninja competitor, executive and life coach, motivational speaker, trainer, and owner of Well Done Life LLC

Cell phone: 614.787.8591 (call or text)

Email: chriswarnky@gmail.com

Facebook: welldonelife

Blog: http://cwarnky.wordpress.com

Training as a Ninja

- Attend a Ninja class at Movement Lab Ohio or Ninja Lite class with instructor Chris Warnky when they are offered.
- Ask about personal and individualized one-on-one Ninja Lite training sessions with instructor Chris Warnky.

Want Chris to Speak to Your Group?

Chris is available to speak to groups on a variety of topics including:

- Topics in his ninja books
- Personal refocus times (retreats)
- Leadership and communication topics
- John Maxwell Team leadership materials

Upcoming Books

Chris has a number of additional books currently in the works.

Thirteen percent of initial profits from sales of Chris's books is donated to Mission Aviation Fellowship (MAF), and subsequent profits to MAF and additional charities.

Free Gifts

If you would like to receive any of the following free gifts, please request them at chriswarnky@gmail.com:

- A short video greeting from Chris with a bonus ninja training experience story
- A bonus story about Chris's 2017 ninja league announcing experience

Be Mentored by Chris Using the 12 Traits of a Ninja

Chris offers "Twelve Trait Mentoring" (from his book *The Heart of a Ninja*), which has been especially ideal for young people who love *American Ninja Warrior* and can benefit from a strong male presence in their lives. Sessions can be conducted in person, by phone, or via Facetime. Choose from 30-, 45-, and 60-minute sessions.

Be Coached by Chris

Chris provides both life coaching and executive coaching.

Acknowledgments

I'm thankful to our awesome Creator/God for allowing me to live my first 62 years and for providing me with many great relationships and experiences. I'm also thankful to have peace with Him because of the life and sacrifice of His Son, Jesus.

Thanks to my wife, Carolyn, for your love and especially for your support while I have been writing, editing, and publishing this and other books. I can't imagine going through anything without you by my side to celebrate our successes and support me in my times of failure and disappointment. I love you!

There are so many others I'm thankful to because of their contributions to my life and/or for their specific help with the writing, editing, and feedback on this book. Below are a few of them:

Thanks to my mom and dad for all the love and support you have provided throughout my life. Thanks to Tim and Bonnie for your love and support. Thanks to Michelle for continually supporting me during my ninja journey.

Thanks to my Lunch Time Training Partners (LTTPs), Shanon Paglieri, Katie Tennant, Scott Walberry, Shea Stammen, Chad Kohler, and Rex Alba, and others who have supported me as we train and compete together. Thanks also to so many other MLAB OH ninjas I train with, including Karen Mead, Seth Newton, and Stephanie Van Schaik. I love spending time with you all.

I'm very thankful for all the great support and instruction provided by the MLAB OH instructors, especially those who have been there for so many open gyms and ninja classes. These include head instructors Jesse Wildman, Kyle Wheeler, Justin Allen, Drake Stevens, and Sophia Oster. You add so much value to my training and for so many others. I appreciate you.

Thanks to Shanon Paglieri and Bryce LaRoche for allowing me to share their ninja action photos on the cover of this book.

Thanks to the many ninjas across the country who have welcomed me and embraced me into your community. Thank you for the encouragement, support, and friendship, and the tips you've shared to make me a better ninja. I appreciate you.

Thanks to Gwen Hoffnagle, my professional editor for my first five ninja books. You have taken my original manuscripts to new and much higher levels. I enjoy working with you and appreciate the value you provide. I would recommend you to any author. Thank you so much! I really appreciate you.

About the Author

Chris Warnky is 62 years young and has been married to Carolyn May Warnky for over 40 years. He has two children: Tim, who lives in Cleveland with his wife, Bonnie, and two daughters; and Michelle, who lives in Columbus and is a popular multi-year *ANW* competitor and a serious, competitive obstacle-course racer.

Chris is an active, training ninja warrior dedicated to his Lunch Time Training Partners. He is also an MLAB OH Ninja Lite instructor and offers personal one-on-one ninja-lite-level targeted training sessions.

He competed in the 2017 *ANW Cleveland City Qualifier* and has competed in numerous ninja competitions over the past couple of years including both National Ninja League and Ultimate Ninja Athlete Association competitions. He provided the play-by-play for numerous Facebook Livestream ninja competitions, including the World Ninja League finals.

Chris has been a Bible-reading Christian for over 50 years. His relationship with God is the basis for his life.

He is an author with plans to write several additional books, a professional executive and life coach, and a thought-provoking speaker through his business, Well Done Life. He coaches clients addressing important life and business topics.

Chris is a certified coach, speaker, and trainer with the John Maxwell Team. He served two years on the organization's President's Advisory Council. He served two terms as the International Coach Federation Columbus Charter Chapter president. He achieved the Toastmasters International "Competent Communicator" designation.

Chris has over three decades of corporate leadership experience, including 23 years as a vice president at Bank One/JP Morgan Chase contributing as a project manager, program manager, and compensation manager.

www.ingramcontent.com/pod-product-compliance
Lightning Source LLC
Chambersburg PA
CBHW071831020426
42331CB00007B/1682